VROOM!
HOW A CAR ENGINE WORKS FOR KIDS

Starting a car is as simple as turning a key. But have you ever wondered what really happens? Every car has an engine below the hood.

An engine is a machine that uses many different parts to convert fuel into energy, or power. An engine creates enough power to make the car move.

Just like your body converts food into energy to move, a car engine converts gasoline into motion. Some newer cars, known as hybrids, also use electricity from batteries. Some get energy from the sun, using solar panels.

When your body
needs fuel, you feed
it food. When your
car needs fuel, you
"feed" it gasoline.
The process of
converting gasoline
into power is
called "internal
combustion".

Internal combustion engines use tiny and controlled explosions to generate the power. It is needed to move your car. A car engine creates explosions hundreds of times per minute.

CAMSHAFT

CAM

MIXTURE IN

INTAKE VALVE

COMBUSTION CHAMBER

CYLINDER BLOCK

CONNECTING ROD

CRANKSHAFT

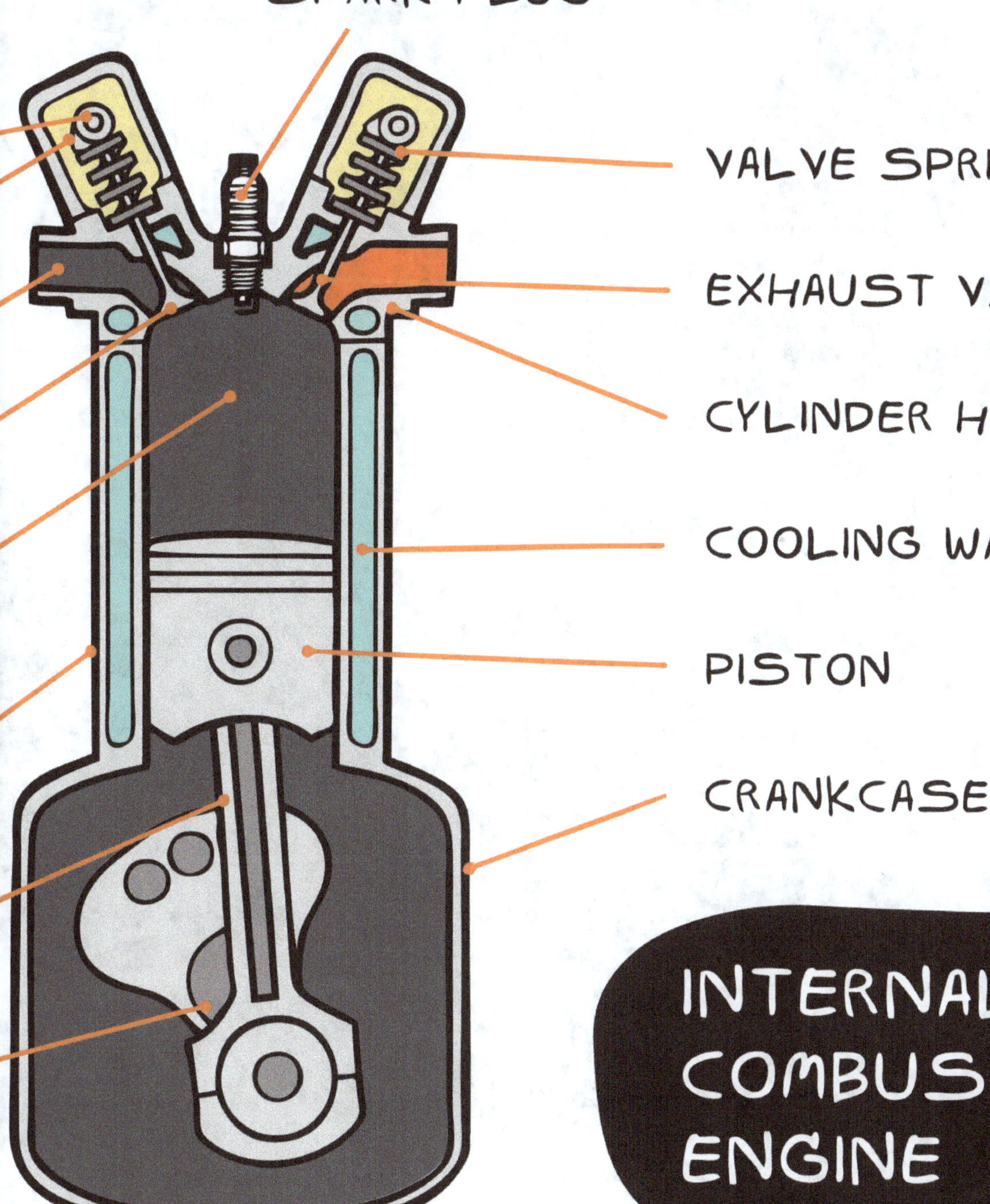

SPARK PLUG
VALVE SPRING
EXHAUST VALVE
CYLINDER HADE
COOLING WATER
PISTON
CRANKCASE
INTERNAL COMBUSTION ENGINE

The engine then
takes the energy
released and uses it
to power your car.

The explosions
forces pistons in
the engine to move.
When the energy
from the first
explosion has used
up, a new explosion
occurs. This powers
the pistons to
move continuously
until it becomes a
cycle giving the car
the power needed
to run.

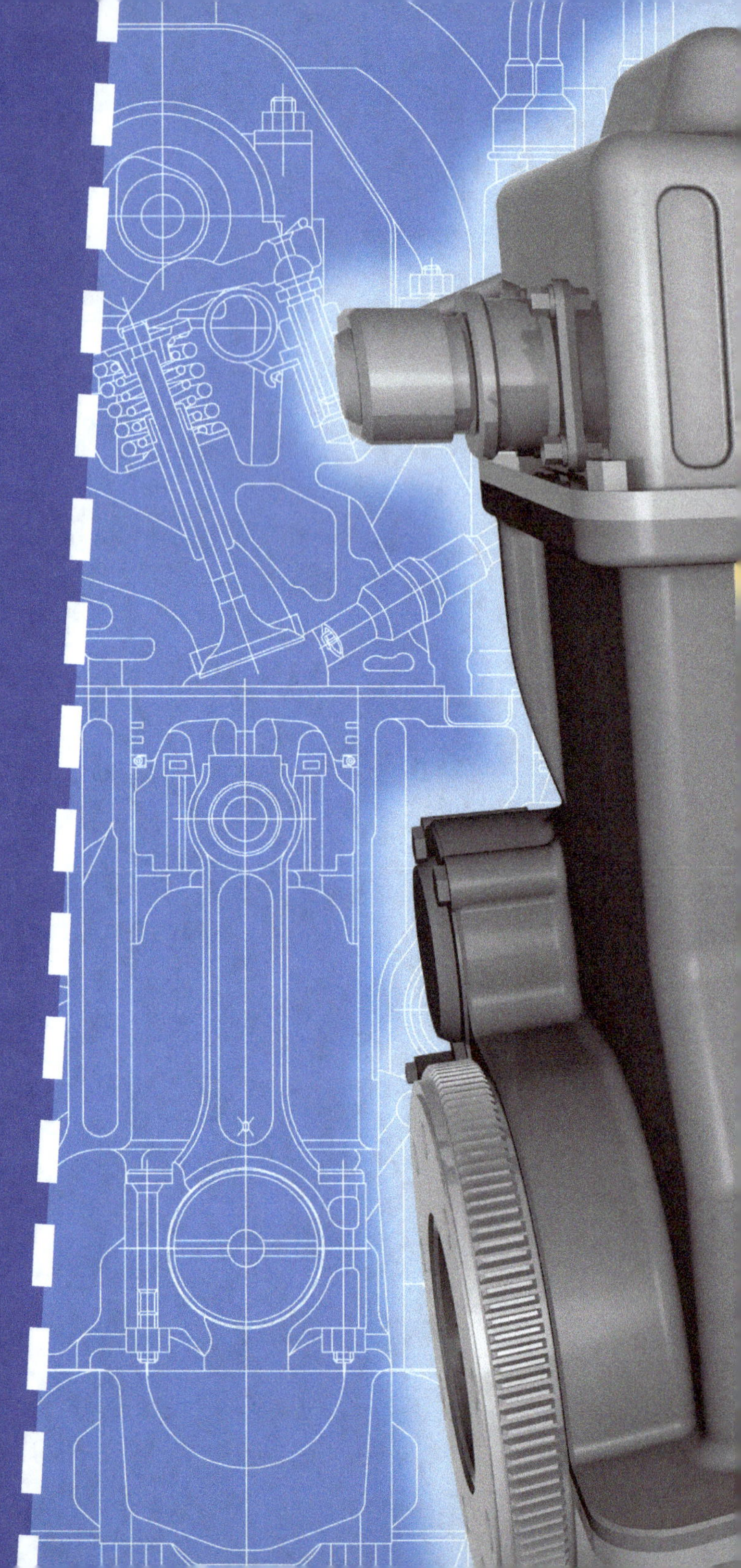

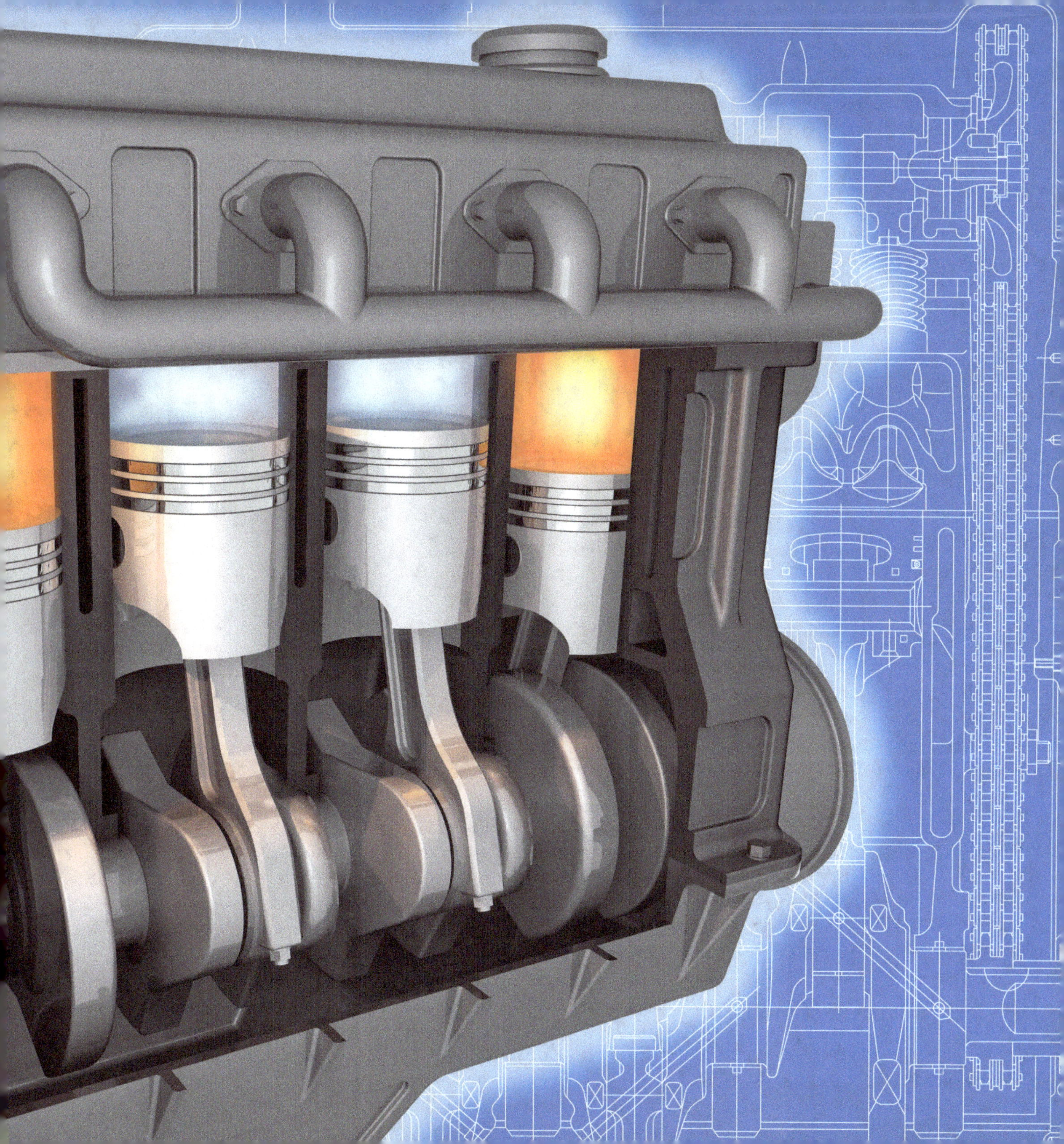

A car engine is a very efficient machine. It burns fuel in containers, which are closed. It holds a major part of the heat energy released by the fuel, and turns it into mechanical energy that drives the car along.

Here are main parts
of a car engine.

Cylinders – They
are made of super-
strong metal and
locked, but they
open and close like
bicycle pumps: they
have tight-fitting
pistons that can
slide up and down
inside them.

They are built around a set of "cooking pots". The fuel burns inside the cylinders.

Pistons — are small parts inside the cylinders. The piston's function is to move up and down. By making this movement, the piston pulls a mixture of gasoline and air into the cylinder and then compress it back up toward the spark plug.

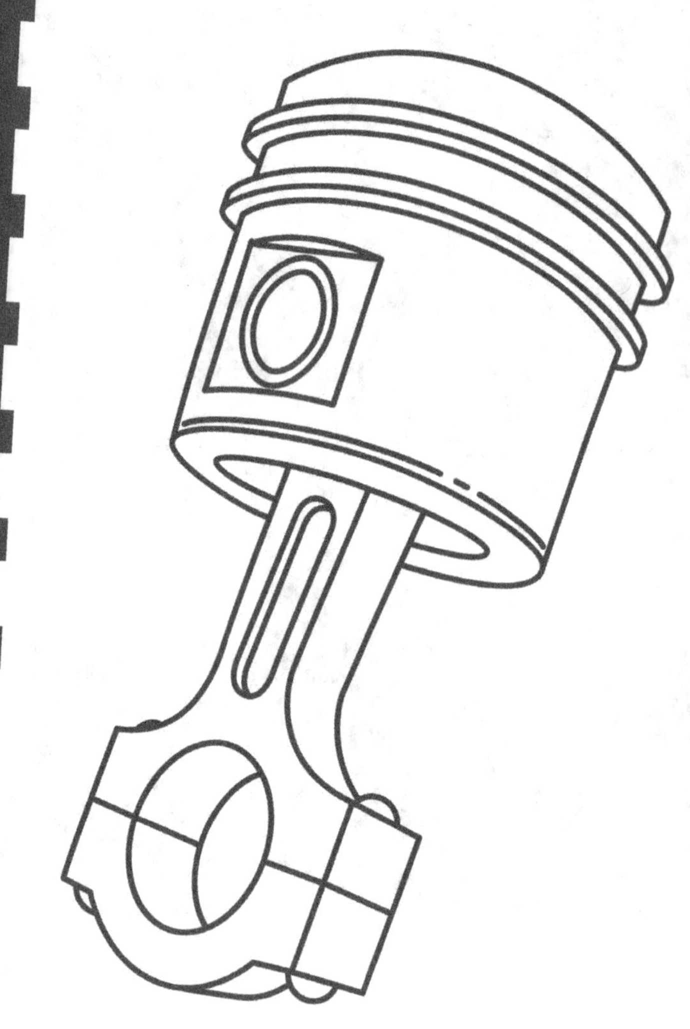

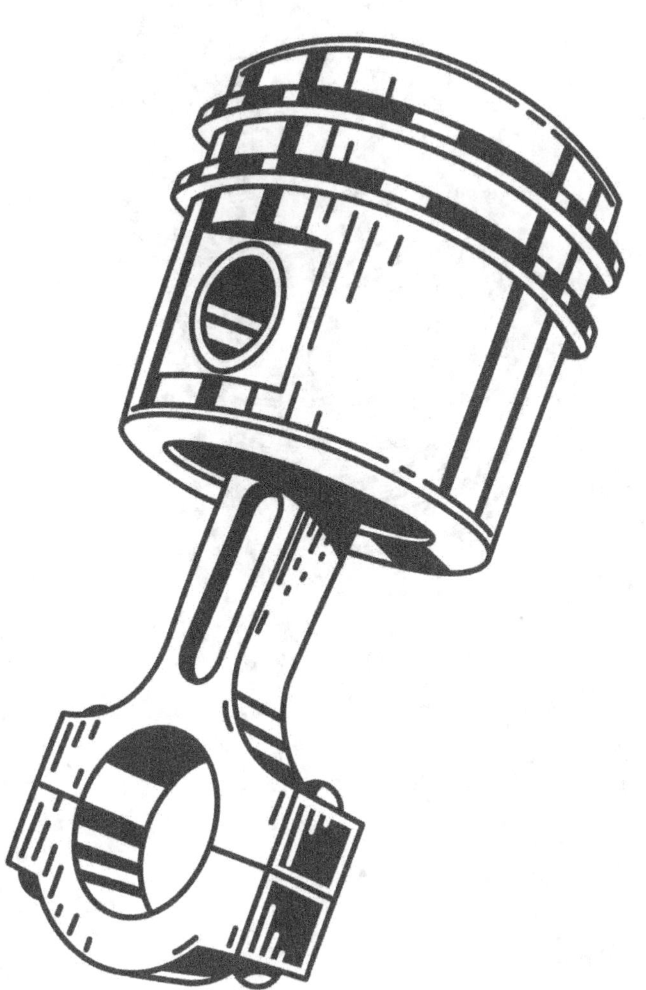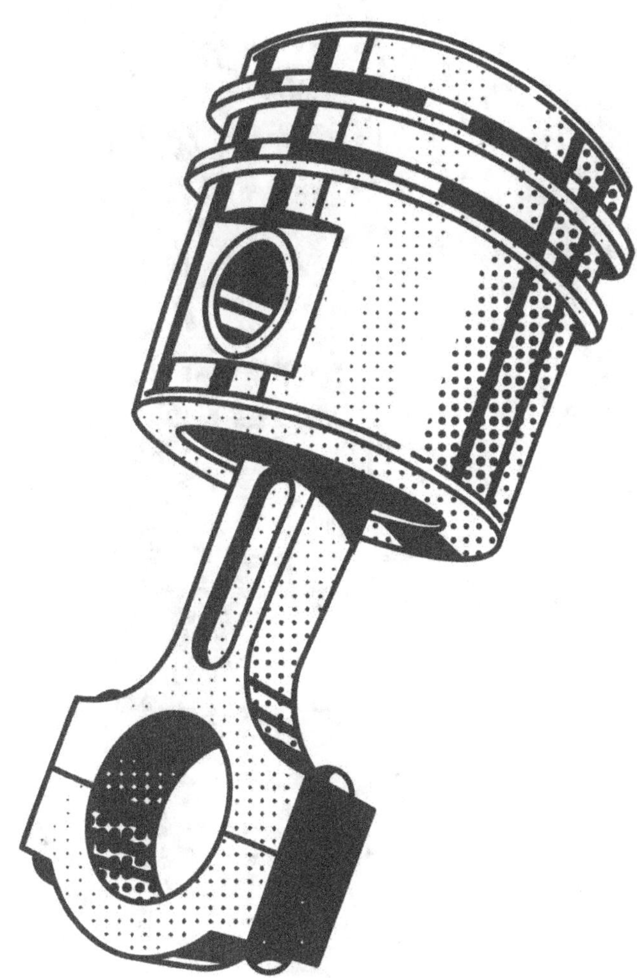

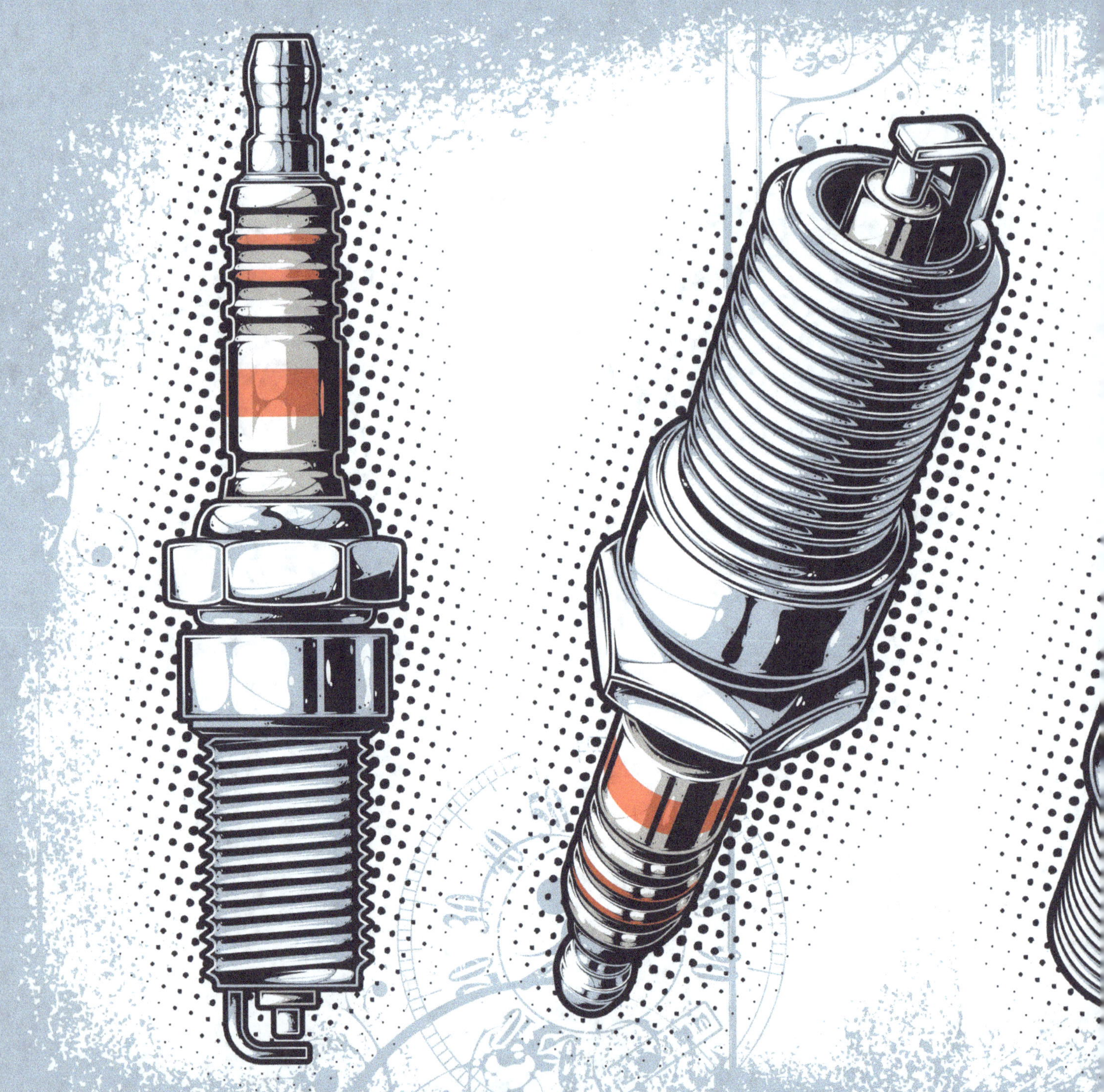

Spark Plug –
The spark plug's function is an electrically controlled device that makes a spark to set fire to the fuel. The resulting explosion creates energy which the engine uses to power the car.

Inlet Valve - It allows a mixture of fuel and air to enter the cylinder from a carburetor or electronic fuel-injector.

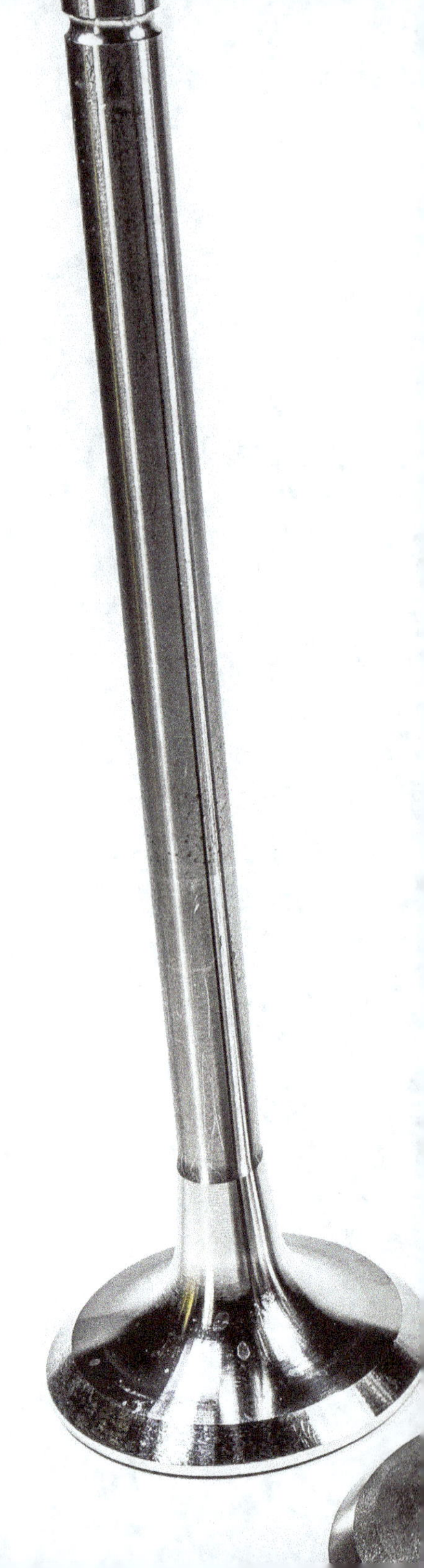

Outlet valve– lets
the exhaust gases
escape.

The flywheel is a large heavy metal disc that is attached to the crankshaft. The fly wheel aids the engine to keep running smoothly. It has teeth that moves by the motor.

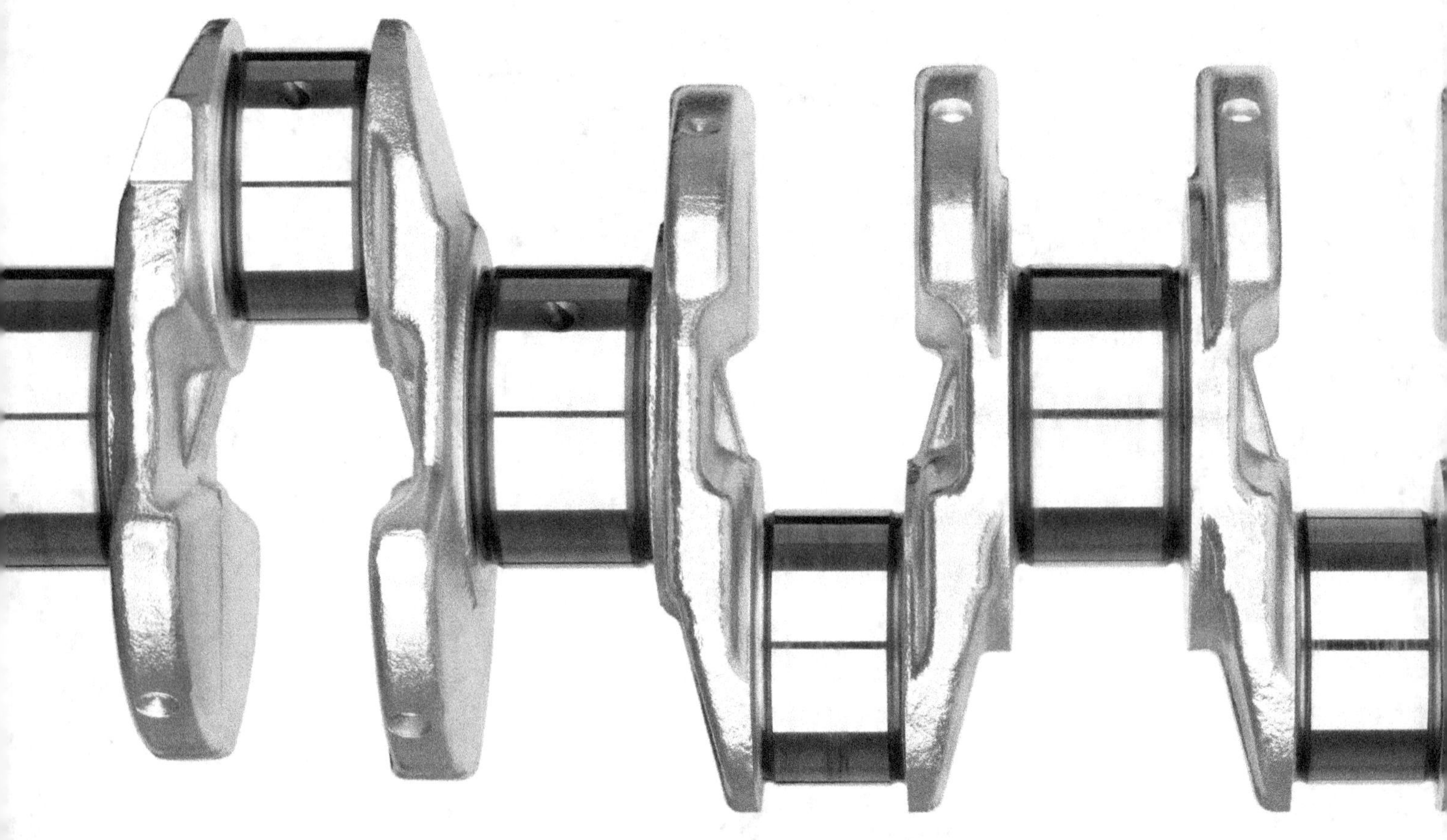

A crankshaft gives and takes energy to many parts of the engine. It moves back and forth as the wheel rotates. The crankshaft is attached to the pistons.

The exhaust gas
pertains to the
gas released
from this entire
process. It is from
the combustion
of fuels like oil,
natural and diesel.
In cars, they are
the gases that
engines give out.

The Engine Cooling System functions by controlling the heat in the car engine. Water is pumped into the passage around the cylinders and then through the radiators to cool down. It prevents the overheating or even burning of your car's engine.

Oil greases parts
of the engine to
allow a smooth
movement. Oil is
pumped out of
a pan that gets
rid of dirt. Oil
also affects the
life of your car's
engine.

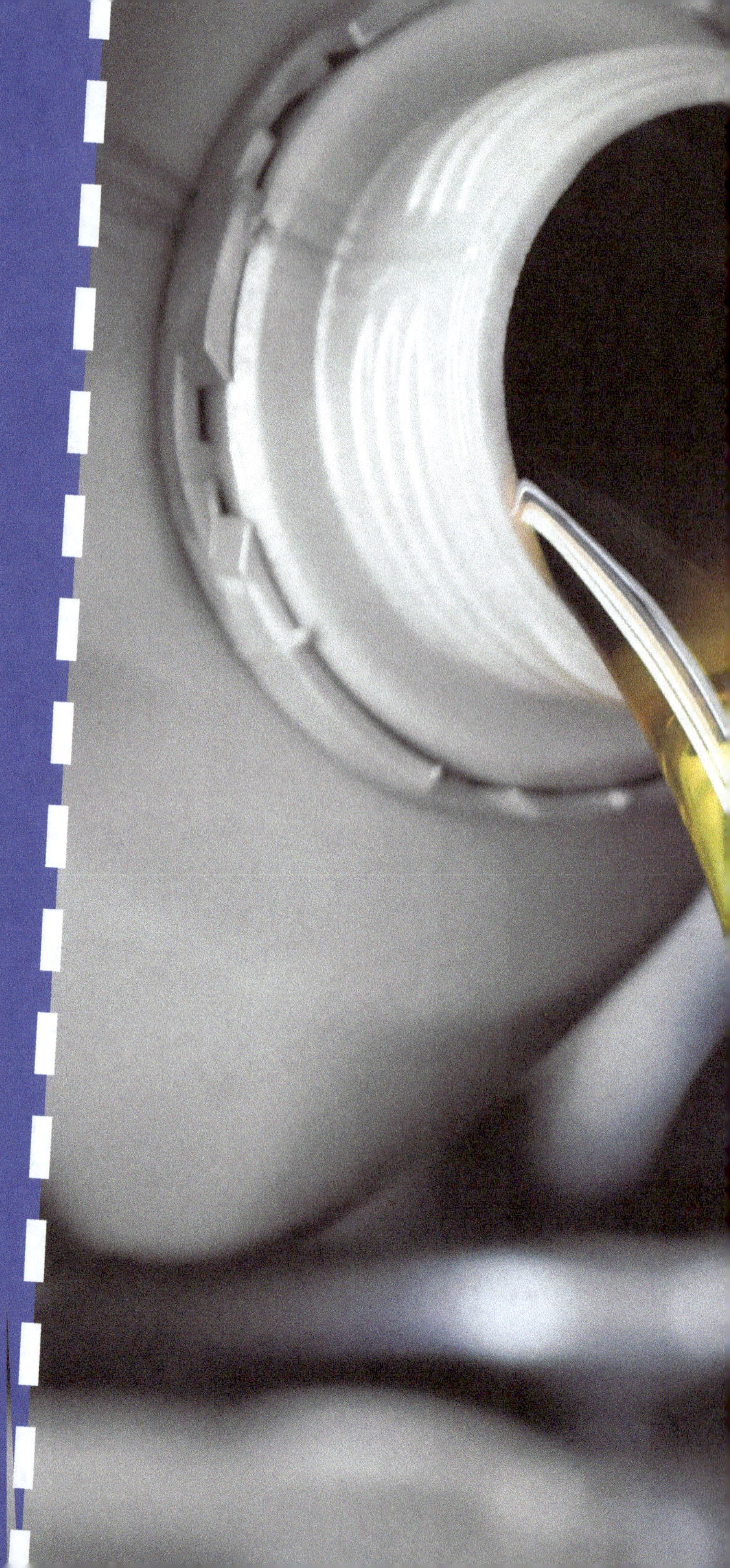

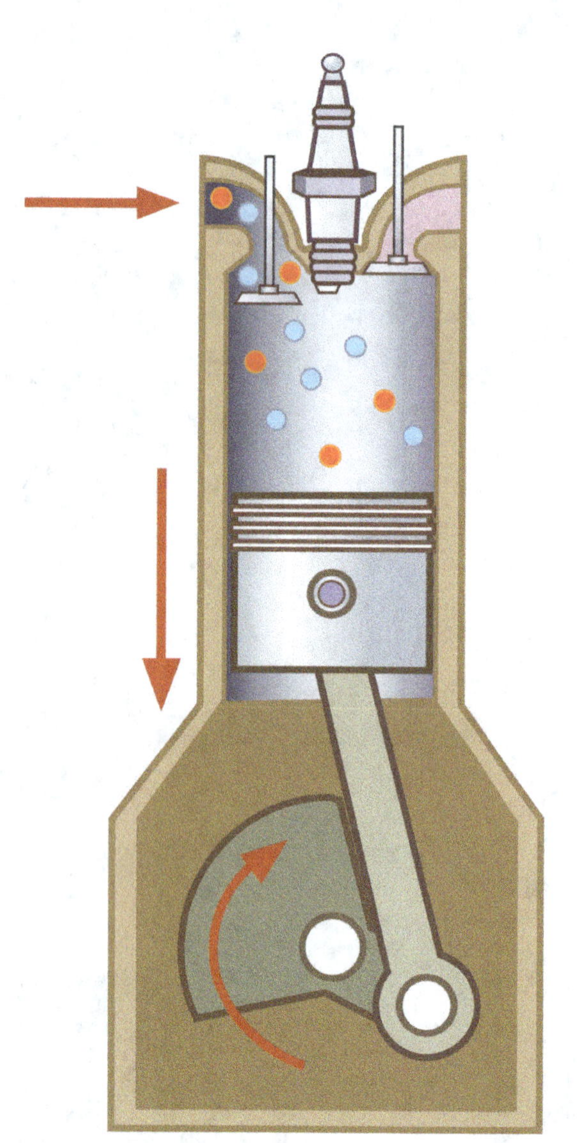
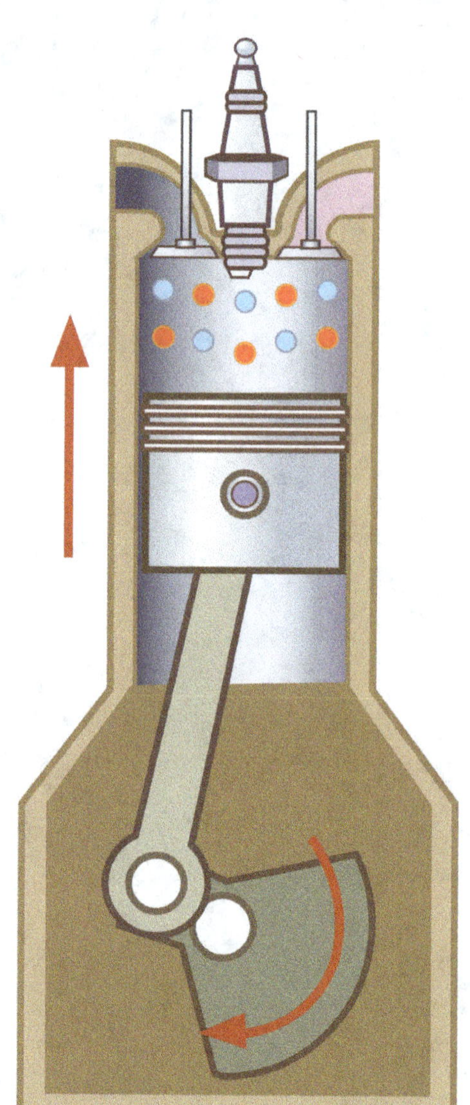
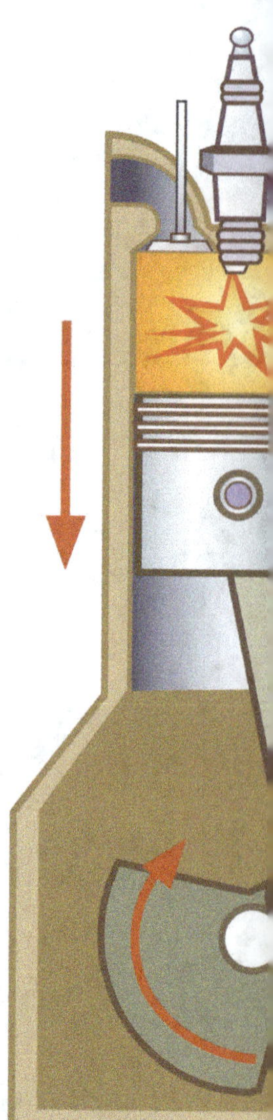

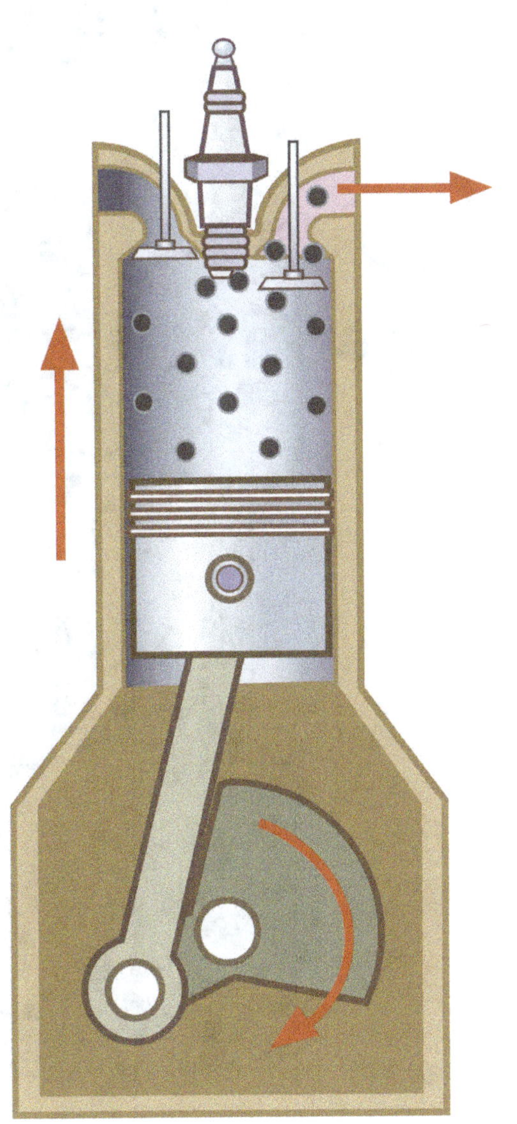

The process of making power in a car engine is an endless repetition. The car works with a four-stroke engine. The strokes are repeated over and over, generating power.

The four strokes of the engine refer to intake, compression, combustion, and exhaust. Let's take a closer look at what happens during each phase.

...ROKE CYCLE ENGINE

FOUR STROKE ENGINE

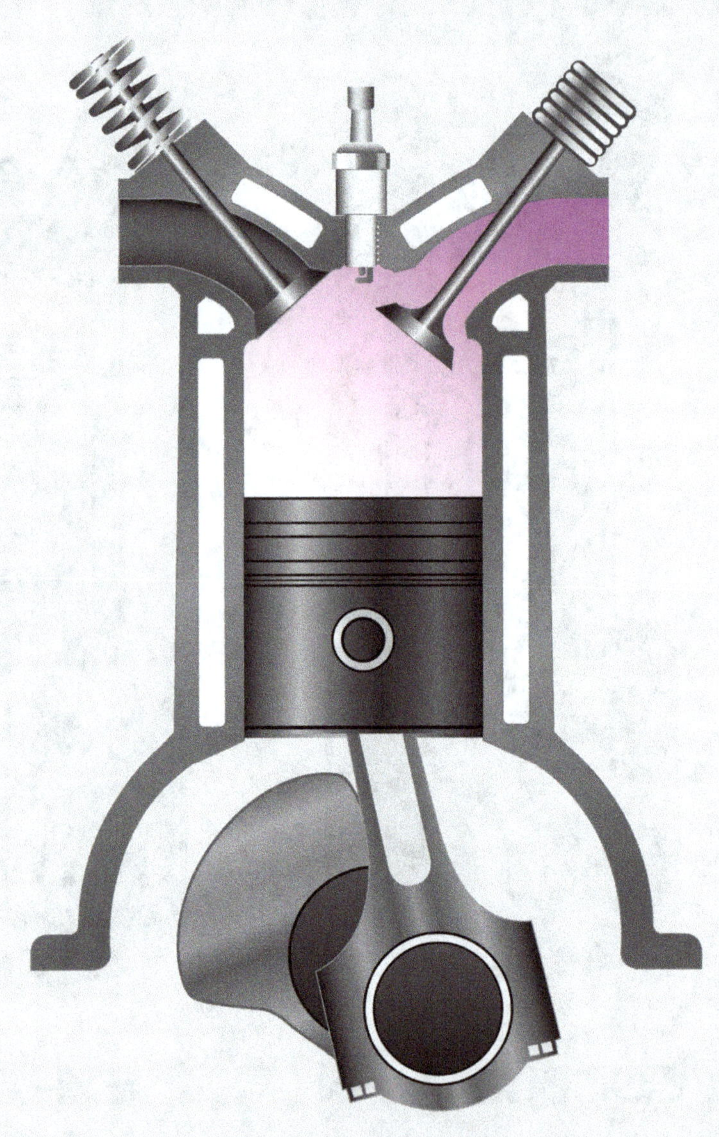

INTAKE

Intake– In the intake cycle, the intake valve opens, and the piston moves down. This begins the cycle by leading air and gas into the engine.

Compression- As the
compression cycle
begins, the piston
moves up and pushes
the air and gas into
a smaller space,
compressing the
mixture. A smaller
space means a more
powerful explosion.

COMPRESSION

FOUR STROKE ENGINE

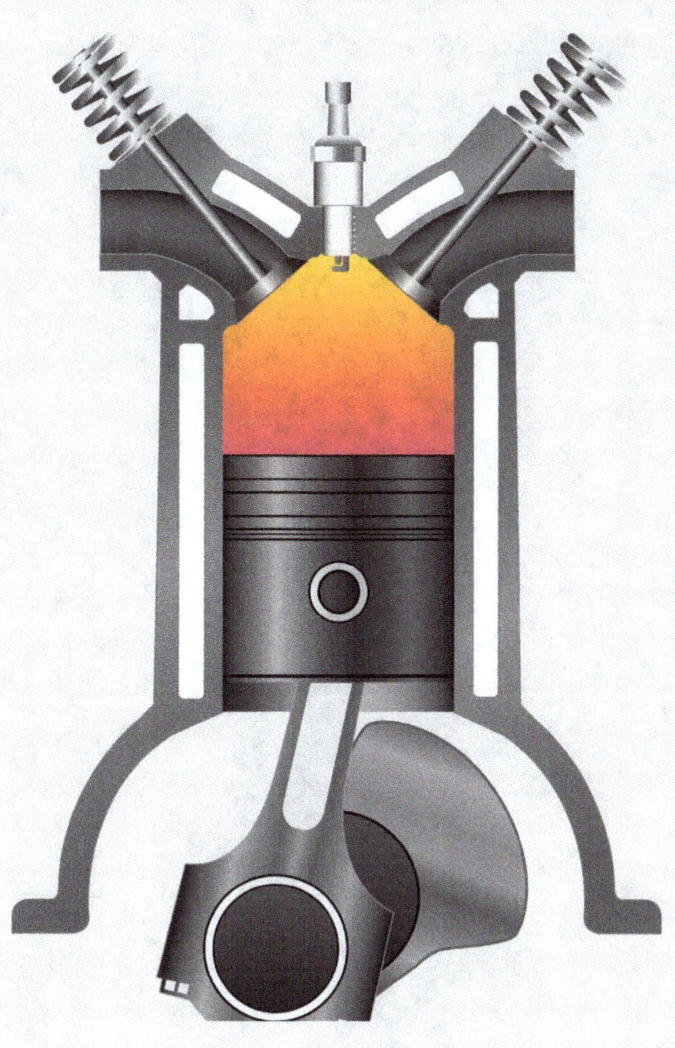

FOUR STROKE ENGINE

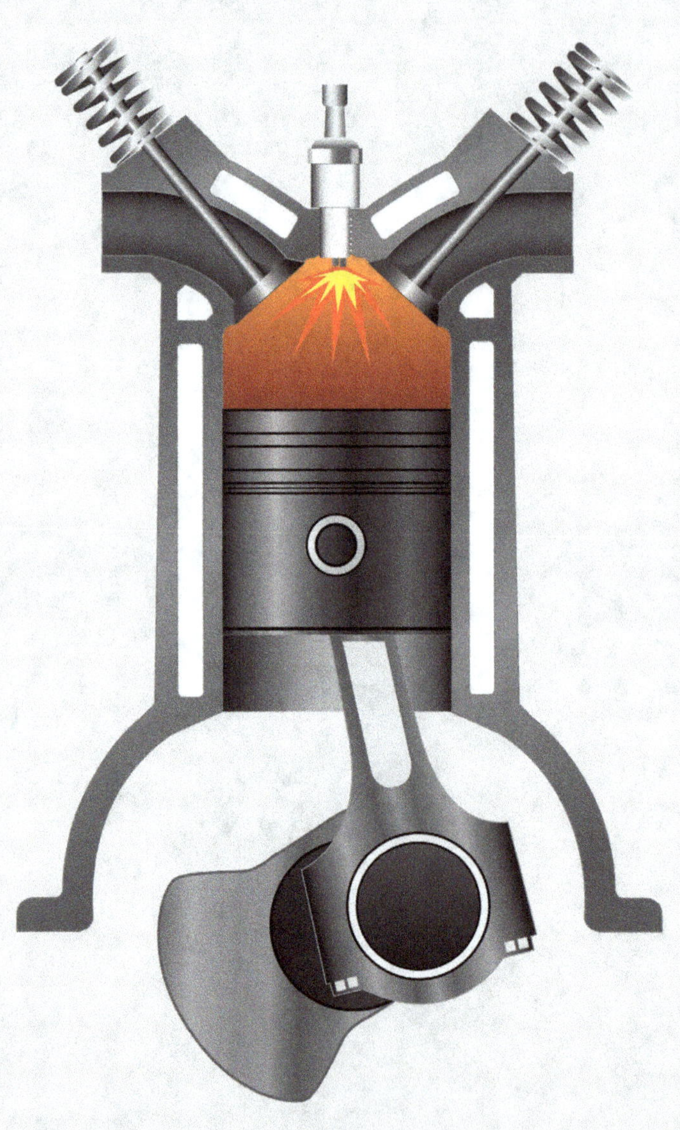

COMBUSTION

Combustion -the spark plug makes a spark that ignites and explodes the gas. The power of the explosion forces the piston back down.

Exhaust-through
the last part of
the cycle, the
exhaust valve opens
to release waste
gas created by
the explosion. This
gas is moved to a
converter, where it
is cleaned, and then
through the muffler
before it exits the
vehicle through the
tailpipe.

EXHAUST

FOUR STROKE ENGINE

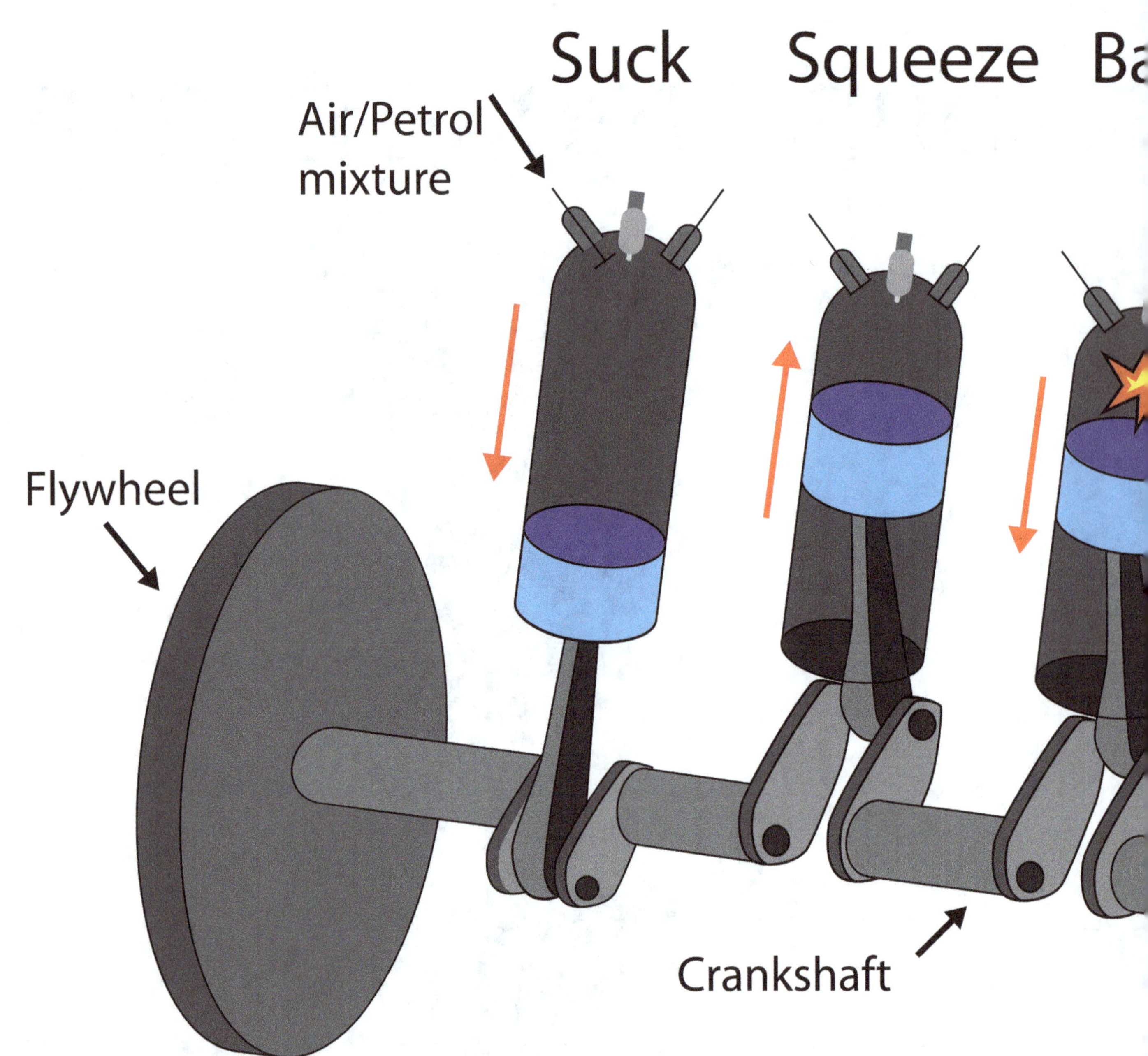

Suck
Squeeze
Ba
Air/Petrol mixture
Flywheel
Crankshaft

Blow

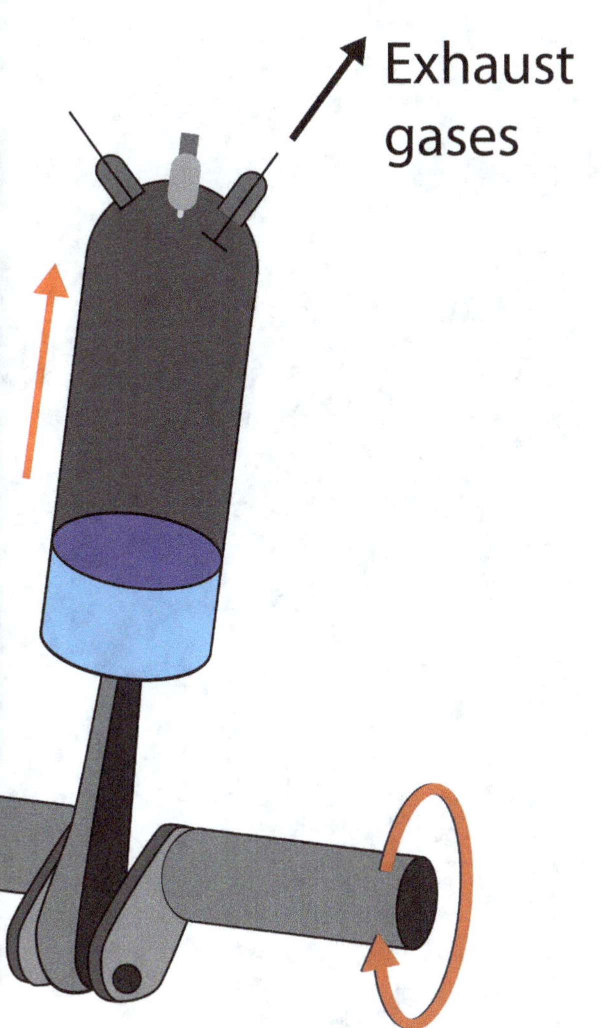

The whole cycle then repeats itself, and with each repetition the car carries you closer to your destination.

Did you know that cars have more than just one piston and valve? If you have more pistons, your car probably is powerful.

Did you know that the world's first automobile was used by the French Army? It was steamed-powered and self-propelled. It was used to move cannons.

Visit
BABY PROFESSOR
EDUCATION KIDS
www.BabyProfessorBooks.com
to download Free Baby Professor eBooks
and view our catalog of new and exciting
Children's Books